Don't Judge a Book by It's Cover

#Recovery Room

SHWANA JAY

New International Version (NIV)
Holy Bible, New International Version®, NIV® Copyright ©1973, 1978, 1984, 2011 by Biblica, Inc.® Used by permission. All rights reserved worldwide.

King James Version (KJV)
Public Domain

Cover by LLA Enterprizes
        Llaenterprizes@gmail.com

Editing by A.T. Destiny Awaits Group LLC
        atdestinyawaitsgroup@gmail.com

DEDICATION

I would like to dedicate this book to my wonderful husband, who gave me the drive to always believe in myself.

To my beautiful daughter, thank you for being the one who made me the woman that I am today.

To my mom, thank you for not getting rid of me because of the way that I was conceived.

To my spiritual advisor, Prophetess Angela Williams who inspired me to get in touch with the spirit within and to always stay focused on where God was taking me and to never look back from where he brought me from..

I dedicate this book to all that come in contact with it. I pray that it heals you and gives you that drive to get closer to God because with God everything is possible through him.. I love you all
#RECOVERYROOM
#THEJAYSWAY

THE SUBSTANCE THAT MATTERS

Acknowledgements.. i

Introduction... 1

The Moment God Spoke 4

When I finally let Go & Let God
  The Chains Broke..............................9

Stay in the Race 21

Your Storm was Designed to Push You............ 24

When It is for You 29

God gets All the Glory..............................31

While in the Valley....................................35

When you are seeking God for Change 37

My Pain had Purpose.................................49

Recovery Room.......................................54

My Prayer for Fatherless Daughters and Sons......56

My Prayer for You....................................58

ACKNOWLEDGEMENTS
MY SPECIAL THANK YOU'S

First and Foremost, I give Thanks to God above. He is the head of my life and who made everything possible when I couldn't see it.

I want to thank my husband Sherod Jay. He has had my back through all my ups and downs.

I give thanks to my one and only daughter Ke'Yanna Wells because without her coming into this world. I would have never known what strength and love was all about.

I want to thank my Spiritual advisor Angela Williams. She has labored with me on this journey.

I want to thank my mom Mary Langston for keeping me.

I really would like to thank Tyeshia Thomas and Que'Nona Valentine Guilford. God landed this right on time. Blessings to you both for giving me the drive that I have inside to pour out in this book and my ministry.

I'm in tears right now because I don't have enough Thank you's to give our Father for making us all in his own image. I love you all and thank you all for supporting the vision God has birthed from within me.

God Bless you all and Thank you again.

Love Always,

Prophetess Shwana Jay

INTRODUCTION

Your story may not be my story, but we have all been through something to be able to say, "God, in spite of it all, you still have a plan for me."

When you are going through for the things man have condemned you for, but they wonder how you are still standing, it is because God still has his hands on you.

No matter where you are on this earth if you don't get to know God for yourself, then you are just walking here on this earth. There isn't a pastor, preacher, evangelist, nor prophet that can lay hands on you to bring you up and fill you with the Holy Ghost. You got to want the King of Glory. Hallelujah, without the King of Glory, you are just here like a bad fruit, that's been eaten up by worms with your flesh eating away at your spirit.

If you are in a spiritual battle, choose to let the spirit win and the flesh die daily. There's nothing too hard for God here on earth. Nehemiah 4:6-19 teaches us that God built towns to separate the women and men of God with children also. The walls were built.

My daily prayer is Keep me oh Lord from my iniquity that I return no more. I have fallen short of the commandments of your law, my God, but straightaway, I will continue to serve you with my whole heart and with love for your people that want you. Teach me, God, Teach me. Amen

Be according to God's word and understand that it will heal and deliver you on days the Lord has made.

I clearly heard the voice of God say, "When my people study my word to show their selves approved; I will teach them how to go. My word is a cleanse like no other medicine. It can heal and deliver you all. Take heed that you will read it, eat it, and get full on it. Understand that I have no respect of persons. Who shall receive the gift and power I give if you don't want to work hard for it? Nothing comes easy. You can't serve me and man. Let not your heart be troubled, in the time of need. I will provide for you all. I will stand for you all that believe and trust in me for I am a spirit that dwells in you. You trust in me to handle your life and shall live and not die. Know life is not your own. I can come like a thief in the night and your breath is gone. Get your house in order, which is your heart, your mind, your soul, and your spirit that you can do my will and I will give you eternal life, abundant life. Your wildest dreams will come true. I hold the power in my hands. What you ask in my Son, Jesus' name, you will receive. Turn away from not just your wicked ways, but from all wickedness. This is I that speak to you on this day that I made. Lift up your chin, take up your bed and continue to be about your Father's business."

Your gift will make room for you!

THE MOMENT GOD SPOKE

I remember it like it was yesterday. On December 5, 2017, I heard my Savior say, "When everybody seems like they are against you, clap your hands, stomp your feet, and take a spin because it's alright. The world can't do anything without Me. The whole world is in My hands, and they will not rule My world."

People look and are amazed now that I have turned you around. Step into boldness. The enemy cannot stop what I have ordained. Yes, you have a past of drugs, clubbing, drinking, stealing, and laying up with men to care for your need. When you learned about the power of my gift, you turned away and never looked back. The hills are high, but the sky is the limit. Keep looking up. You are the apple of my eye. The love I have for my people will never change, but I will not let them rule nations with their immoralities.

The weather changes, seasons change, time changes, people change, things change, but God's hands never change. Hold on to

God's unchanging hands. He is going to lighten up your heavy loads. It won't be like this always. You can trust the process in God's words, "Keep pushing, it gets real day by day." Day by day, here is what you have to do Pray, Pray, Pray. When the odds are stacked against you, just fall to your knees and begin to call on Jesus.

I didn't want the life that God had given me because of everything I went through. I turned to drugs and alcohol because of the pain. I would love to blame it on the world, but it wasn't the world, it was me doing the things that were of the world.

John 15:19 states, "If ye were of the world, the world would love his own: but because ye are not of the world, but I have chosen you out of the world, therefore the world hateth you."
(KJV)

God is trying to teach you how to be the student, while he remains the teacher, and yes, it is hard.

Growing up, it was very hard for me to forgive or to say I'm sorry to someone. At the age of 5, I was molested by my stepfather.

This went on until I was 12 years old. Knowing that God had his hands on me, and he loved me like none other kept me.

Growing up with hate in your heart is of the enemy. The enemy robbed me of love. When I came home from school, I used to want to play all day, so I wouldn't have to go into the house with him. Knowing he would wait until the lights were out and he would crawl in there to my bed. I would just lie there like I was sleep asking the Lord to please make him stop.

See grace and mercy will see you through even the most terrible times. I grew up an angry, bitter woman, not knowing where I should be or what I should be doing in life. When I thought God didn't love me because of what I went through, it was comforting to know that he kept his hands on me. I believed I was too broken to be blessed.

Sometimes you have to suffer to get your breakthrough. "No more tears" is what I would tell myself. Along with the phrase, "It will all be over soon." I've found on this life's journey you have to know that you are justified by faith. Faith gave me just a little push, just a hug, just a smile, just a pure heart, just love, and just faith.

No one will love you like you love you. God created all of us different and everybody's assignment is not the same. Stop getting mad at someone because they complain when you are doing good. I know you feel like they are hating, but surely what a man thinks is in his heart, so is he.

For example, if I like the shoes you purchased, and it's my taste, I will purchase that shoe. We just won't wear it at the same time. If I like the style of car you drive, and I purchase it, we won't drive it at the same time. Our assignments are not designed the same, but God gave us all one. Whether it is to write a book, own your own business, or both. Get on your grind and fulfill your assignment.

As the years went by, anger, bitterness, self-pity, low self-esteem, and all took over at once. I turned to drugs. I was looking for a way out of the pain that I carried from childhood into my adult years. No one knew my pain. I went in and out of jail. My record was so bad that no one would hire me, but when God spoke to me everything changed.

WHEN I FINALLY LET GO AND LET GOD
THE CHAINS BROKE

I should have gotten rid of you. You didn't supposed to be here, your father raped me, and I didn't want him, were only some of the derogatory comments shouted at me by my mother, time and time again.

Growing up can be downright hard, especially when you have a mother that was an alcoholic, and you have been molested by the man you called daddy.

During my childhood every Saturday morning, I would get up before the adults and start breakfast for my siblings. It was four of us kids, but my mom only had three with her. The oldest couldn't go because my great-grandmother wouldn't let him.

I remember the night we left. The fight between my mom and her grandmother that night was very sad. We didn't have time to pack everything we wanted. We just had to take what we needed. To watch my mom, cry the way that she did, hurt me. As I held my little sister, my little brother sat beside me crying, because he saw my mom cry. I didn't want to go because I didn't want to leave my cousins. We were always close to my mom's sister's kids.

Earlier that day while our moms attended an event uptown, my cousins and I were playing outside. I remember it was cold and I was wearing my purple jacket that was torn on the side because I had been in a fight, red hat and gloves. Well anyways, while Jessie and I were playing, I remember hearing my grandmother scream out, "Mae don't come in here with that." We had been playing so hard we didn't know that our moms had made it back from town.

See, my cousins came down every weekend to be with us and left on Sundays. So, this argument was going on that evening at the same time their dad was there picking them up.

During this heated moment between my mom and grandmother, I remember my mom kept saying ya'll want to rule my life and my grandmother was saying ain't nobody tell you to have all them children from different daddy's. See back then, you were talked about in the community if all your kids didn't come from the same man, but my mom wasn't worried about what she was saying. She shouted back, "I take care of my damn kids and take care of ya'll ass too!"

One cold winter morning, we were excited because it was so much ice on the ground that it looked like it had snowed. It was Christmas Eve morning, which was the day before my baby sister turned three months old. We didn't have a home of our own at the time, so we were staying with my grandma, her sister, brother that was ill, and my great grandmamma.

I remember my grandmother's brother's illness was so bad that it caused him to moan and groan all night because of the amount of pain. I still remember my auntie warming water so that he could put his feet in it to soothe him.

I remember one night my baby brother, the one who always followed me around, in everything I did crawled down the hall to the room in the back. That room used to be my auntie's room, but because my uncle was dying, her and my great grandma was sleeping in the living room on the let-out bed. My oldest brother Skip slept with my auntie Dolly. I slept with my grandma Wilma. Every night before bed everyone had to say their prayers before they laid down.

It was so cold in the house, you would rather be outside then to be in there, but it felt better after you got into my grandma's bed. Which had about twelve blankets and two flat sheets on it. Once you were in, you were in and there was no more moving.

One night, I heard the adults say to one another that my uncle won't make it through the night. My grandma began to pray for her brother, I kneeled beside her and began to pray as well.

Earlier that morning while Uncle Tom was still fighting to live my ma called in my great gran and the prayer warriors. At that time, I didn't know what a prayer warrior was nor did I understand what they could do.

"Prayer warriors," I said. All I could think about was they were going to war and how?

Well, it was four men and three women including ma. They surrounded Uncle Tom's bed and they begin to pray. I sat in the hallway and I can remember crying because of the prayer. I knew then Uncle Tom was really sick. My ma was screaming up and down the hall in the living room sat my mama's mother and sister. She was rocking back and forth.

Suddenly, the prayers stopped, the tears stopped, and he was gone. I watched them as they closed his eyes. My auntie and ma then got up and pulled out some clothes. Ma told my auntie to come and help clean him up. Then, she made a call for the mortuary to pick him up, not knowing what that meant at the time because of being only five years old. I did know about death. They carried him out on a stretcher.

After the funeral, my mom moved, and I cried more because I didn't want to leave grandma and ma. We moved in with my sister's daddy. My oldest brother didn't go. It was just me, Pete and the baby. We left to go be in a small town called Baker County with my sister's father.

There we were in this Big house with lots of rooms and the school was great. Then everything changed and life got complicated.

I grew up in a home with my mom, two brothers and one sister. I was the second oldest my mom moved from Damascus out from around her mom when I was five.

See, we all had different fathers All three of my siblings knew their dads, but I didn't. My mom always told me that I wasn't supposed to be here because my father raped her.

During the time of moving here and there my mom was an alcoholic and stepfather was too. The late-night fights at our house would start between mama and my stepfather after they had gone out and had a good time. I could hear my mom screaming and I would get up to go rescue her. She would beg him not to fight her in front of me (giggles). I could remember holding my mother. Then, she would push me off and tell me it was my fault.

We resided in Ft. Pierce, Florida. That's when my life turned upside down in 1981. It started on a Saturday night. My sister's daddy asked me to sit on his lap. I still remember what I was wearing. I had on my red and white lace dress, white socks, and my little black shoes. We had been to see ma and grandma. Mama always was getting into it with them about me. Ma (my grandmother) would yell I don't trust him! Five years old, I was molested by my stepfather and it went on until I was twelve. I used to lie in bed and wish I was dead because I didn't have anyone to talk to about it. I told God to please make him stop. I can remember one Saturday night my grandma called and told my mom that she had a dream about my stepfather doing all types of things to me, boy my heart dropped because I had told it one day to my auntie when I talked to her on the phone. My mom was so angry with me. I remember her making me get under the dinner table and pray and ask God to forgive me for lying.

By the time we moved back to Georgia beside my grandma I was this little girl that's all mature butt, titties, and everything. When I was just 13 years old grown men thought I was 18. I begin to act out in school.

So again, there I was thirteen years old with the scars from having been molested from age five to twelve. All I wanted was someone to love me and to care for me. I just wanted someone to tell me that I was worth it and mean it, but I was still hearing my mother's voice telling me that it was my fault and she shouldn't have never had me.

As time progressed, I started sneaking out of the window with grown men that would take me off, have sex with me and then pay me for it. I would have money in school and at home. My mom never knew about it. This went on for years, throughout Highschool until I became a drop out my 12th grade year.

In 1991 my whole life changed. That was the year that I ran away from home to be with a man triple my age. This was a man that would soon start to abuse me physically and emotionally. In other words, I left school to be with the man that would slap me around anytime he wanted, pull my hair, and drop me on my neck. I ran away from home with him because he said he loved me and would take care of me.

Life was already hard. See, when you come from a family of four, with no father, and all the children has different daddies. Not to mention a mother that tried to drink away her problems and not deal with the fact that she had a child that had been molested. To top it off, she blamed that child for him touching her from the time she was five years old until she was twelve. Well, I was that child and I took that abuse.

So, needless to say at 15 I wasn't a virgin because my virginity was taken by my stepfather. So yes, I ran away with the first guy that said he loved me. It didn't matter that I was 15 living from house to house with a 28-year-old man and barely going to school. He told me he loved me and that was more than I can say for many others in my life.

Although my mom came everyday begging me to come home I wouldn't because

I felt free as a grown up. Until one night that man that I thought loved me slapped me so hard from the kitchen to the hallway because the food was cold. I remember doing all I could to satisfy him because I felt like he loved me. He would apologize and I would stay. It felt like weeks would go by with no whooping, but then it became the norm for Wednesdays, Fridays, and Sundays. This continued until I was 17.

By that time, he was committing crimes so drastic and I knew if he went to jail, I would be free. We had to hide out for a month. He kept me hostage and sent me and his grandma to the store whenever we needed food. Yes, I know you may be asking, "Why didn't I leave?" It was because every time I left he told me, "If you try anything I will kill your family." So, I didn't try. When the law finally came and caught him they took me too. I went to jail for hiding a fugitive.

There I was 17 years old and wondering, "What is really going on?" My mom hadn't seen me in 2 years, but I found myself behind bars, scared, and needing her. I had never been in anything like that before.

I know God hears your cries, so I cried out to him. I was released in my mom's care, but I couldn't leave the state. I was like God what is going on?

A year went by and there I was in front of a judge, alone. My mom was still angry because I left. At this point, I was standing there not really believing there was a God, even though I had grown up in the church all my life. When I swayed, I remembered listening to the Pastor speak about God turning his back on you, and that's what I thought God had did. The bigger the disappointment equals the bigger the blessings, and the more they hurt you the bigger the reward.

I gave birth to my only child, a baby girl, August 25, 1995, and I vowed to God that I would protect her with everything within me. What happened to her? Well, her father, who was never needed in her life, left the day she was born. So, there I was again heartbroken, homeless, no job, living house to house with people I thought were my friends and everything my mom said he would do, he did it.

She didn't lie. Now, she had problems with drinking but if you came to the house and she said you ain't right most of the time she was telling the truth.

A word of encouragement: If you are in an abusive relationship right now, don't stay! If he hit you once, don't stay! He will do it, again. If you have children, don't do it for them do it for you. Let God be your guidance. Whether it's physical or emotional because words will tear you down.

The old saying sticks and stones may break my bones, but words will never hurt is a lie! Words will hurt you. They will cut so deep that you might not heal if you don't learn how to let go and let God.

STAY IN THE RACE

I had a newborn baby, on a one-year probation and had to pay a fine, no job but if I could go that year without getting into any trouble at all that would all come off my record.

I started dating the man I am currently married to July 6,1996. This was a man that had chased me for six years. He was a drug dealer. So needless to say, he took great care of me and my daughter financially.

As years went by, I was let down by friends, family, the man that I had deeply fell in love with and jobs with no one to turn to, I was introduced to drugs by my homeboy in 1998 to ease my pain. I found myself in and out of jail for fighting. Nothing mattered not even my child, the one I brought in this world. I was in and out of Church because I wasn't ready to do God's will.

I was dealing with some serious trust issues because I knew this man was different from the one before because he found himself in the arms of another woman but claimed to still love me. But even through our ups and downs I chose to stay because there were some issues that I had to still deal with within myself.

Although this man saw my scars, I failed to let him in close enough to understand my heart, nor had I been able to trust him with my past hurt and pain. So needless to say, we were both to blame.

While still in the race, God still saw fit to join us together in Holy Matrimony on July 6, 2011. Thinking things could get better because God honored marriage, but I wasn't living how God wanted so we struggled. I was still using drugs and clubbing every weekend. My daughter was left to raise herself.

In 2014 I decided that I was tired of running. Prophetess Angela Williams came into my life and through her God turned my life around. The attacks got bigger, but the blessings were well worth it. God blessed my marriage. We both got into Church. He lost his job of thirteen years. I lost my job of fifteen years, but God opened bigger and better doors. He is a CDL truck driver and I am a Phlebotomist.

We chose to stay in the race and God blessed us both with great careers. Not to mention my husband was able to get his driver's license back after 20 years.

Romans 8:4, KJV proclaims, "That the righteousness of the law might be fulfilled in us, who walk not after the flesh, but after the Spirit."

I learned to kill my flesh daily, and still have to, now. Never stop asking God to renew your mind. Your mind got to be made up to serve the Lord. Stay in the race.

Psalm 121:5, KJV, assures, "The Lord is thy keeper: the Lord is thy shade upon thy right hand."

YOUR STORM WAS DESIGNED TO PUSH YOU

When we learn to stop focusing on what the storm has taken us through, we can focus on the purpose we are here for, and it didn't kill you because God has you here for a reason. Your storm is a part of your past, so let the past be the past, and let God, get you to your greater.

Suddenly, I found myself in a place where I didn't know where my life was headed, nor did I understand what my purpose on earth was; I just knew I wanted and needed a change. I wanted more of God and less of myself. I couldn't live that way anymore.

I was thinking about so much the day I let God into my life. On that day, I met a woman that taught me about the Holy Spirit and how to activate my faith. She taught me how to appreciate what God has put in me. See, we are all born with a gift, but there are levels to you living a kingdom life on earth.

John 3:12 states, "If I have told you earthly things, and ye believe not, how shall ye believe, if I tell you of heavenly things?"

I took God's hand and let him show me how to live here on earth before I can get to heaven. I knew I needed God, and I just didn't want him, I had to have him.

Many days I struggled with my past, and it kept me from going farther. The enemy would play with my mind. See, I quit everything cold turkey, and it was hard. I was under attack daily on my job, in my home, in the Church, and within myself. The anointing oil on our lives cost. I had to go through the fire because I surrendered to God. I didn't give God half of me; I gave him all of me.

There I was in a storm, married to the love of my life and thinking because I gave my life to God, I needed him to do the same. Now, don't think because I had gotten rid of the drugs, alcohol, clubbing, etc. that I still didn't' have issues because I did. I still held on to the root things that were described at the beginning of my story.

When I tell you, I couldn't say I'm sorry because pride had me bound, believe it. I used to bash my husband about the things he was doing by telling him God's going to get you. That was a no, no, and I was wrong because God doesn't deal with us on what we don't let him have, we just won't see his glory like we need to see it, but he will give us mercy because he first loved us.

So again, there I was saved, and delivered but my husband was not. I always listened to other ministers about not being equally yoked. My spiritual advisor was the only on that kept it 1000 with me. Her words alone, "You are NOT God! Just like God did it for you, he will do it for him." Before she would hang up, she would say you need to apologize. You were wrong, and I'm not going to sugar coat it with you. Do you want me to be real or fake? Boy, I use to be pissed, but I obeyed what she was telling me what the spirit of God was speaking to her. It's like they say you can lead a horse to water, but you can't make him drink.

Although this storm was designed to push me, I still battled with these issues for about three years. I went back and forth between my flesh and spirit.

One night, I was awakened up from my sleep and began to pray. God taught me how to be a good wife. He taught me how to take on his mind and empty me of anything that was not of him. I found myself praying, "Forgive me God for all my shortcomings, and I forgive those that came up short concerning me. I remove myself from being in control and give you full control of my life."

I remember going to Church, that Sunday and the Pastor spoke a word over me. At that moment, I begin to shout. I knew what it felt like to catch the Holy Ghost. I don't remember anything other than how the Spirit danced with me. Coming from a Baptist Church, it seemed like you only shouted when you were going through. What they would say was not true because you are shouting to let God in the way he wants you to give him access to you. Shouting is also, to give him the glory for what he will do and what he has already done for you and your family.

When I let go and let God, my marriage got better. I knew how to pray against the enemy. I endured the attacks. I cried tears of joy. I knew how to get my portion with perfect peace. I knew I wasn't perfect, but I was being made perfect by God. Doors opened for me that man said I could never have or enter into, but God is Amazing.

Stay encouraged and know that your storms are designed to push you. People will hate you because of the favor you have on your life and because they are threatened by you.

Remember, never judge a book by its cover. The same person you decide to judge and are jealous of has been granted an anointing that will shift your life. I used to be embarrassed about the things I've had to walk through until I got the revelation that my process was producing an uncommon oil. My anointing cost something. My storms were designed to push me.

WHEN IT IS FOR YOU

Let God be your navigation system. When you have taken the wrong turn, God is navigating you back through a U-turn. He will navigate you back to the right turn.

Growing up, giving up was never an option. No matter what went on in my life and I have experienced everything from having suicidal thoughts at twenty-one, feelings of being incapable of raising my child, not being able to hold on to a job because of being held down by anger and bitterness, being addicted to drugs at the age of 22, and having been molested from the time I was 5 to 12, being told by your mother that I was a mistake baby, and being hurt by my family. I was in and out of trouble and jail. All while, trying to see where this life was taking, but giving up still wasn't an option.

You should Never get mad about the blessings of other folks because you don't know what or how they suffered to get it.

Finally graduating with my High School diploma in May of 2014 was a quick turnaround for me. After being told you will never amount to anything by teachers and people you loved will kind of have you feeling that way about yourself.

When you are chosen by God, no man or woman can stop you. Be led by the spirit and not by what people think. See God said in his word many are called but few are chosen. I thank God for Him choosing me.

I found myself saying, "God, I thank you that when I went through the fire, I didn't come out smelling like smoke." See, I know that the smoke had the ability to kill me before the fire But, God chose me to live. He chose me to live and I can assure you that He will hear your cry. God will hear you confess all. Just have faith and believe it's going to turn around for your good. God is doing it now. Believe in your heart that it is already done, and God won't fail you. Every knee shall bow and every tongue shall confess.

GOD GETS ALL THE GLORY

When you know God loves you in spite of you, it is life-changing, and you realize that God gets all the glory.

At 21 years old, I was a cocaine and marijuana user. I was drinking and going through a pack or two of cigarettes a day. I was a drug addict by the time I turned 22. My life seemed like it was just spiraling out of control, especially when I learned that what happened to me had happened to my daughter. I remember thinking, God just couldn't be letting this happen to me. Why God? I pray I treat people right, but it is you bringing all this back to me.

Well, the use of cocaine, marijuana, drinking, smoking cigarettes ended me up in the hospital because of almost overdosing on it. I was up all-night taking medication to go to bed. I felt like I failed as a mom. I let my little girl down just like my mom did me. I didn't want this to happen. I screamed out to God about how he hated me. I traveled down a road of no return, but God brought me out when I got myself out of the way.

I had to come to a place in my life where I knew that God still deserved to get all the glory. Although I had been molested from the age of five to twelve, God still deserved the glory. Even though I was broken down and damaged mentally by the time I was 15 years old, God still deserves the glory. Even thinking back on every time that I felt the need to run away from home, God still gets all the glory.

I grew up attending church and singing in the choir, but I was bitter from the abuse I suffered at the hands of my stepfather. Although my mom was a drinker, and she put all her troubles in a bottle, I still decree that God deserves all the glory. I always felt if I was never born, she wouldn't be this way. I knew of my father, besides my mom said he raped her to get me, but God still deserves all the glory.

God came to me one day when I was 36. I remember traveling from my hometown to another city. I had been praying that God take the taste from my mouth, yet I continued to do just what I wanted, and it seemed as if God didn't hear me.

So, I was listening to 105.5 radio station and the pastor was preaching about your spiritual baby. I began to shout and push the gas. I passed out with my cigarette in my hand went down in a ditch headed for trees and a light pole. I can hear myself saying why is it dark why can't I see? I can't feel my body, where am I? As I opened my eyes, I could see the spirit of the Lord steering my car as I came all the way through. I was a nervous wreck, but God gets all the glory. It could've been a lot worse.

Sometimes we never know where life may lead us and if we dwell in our past then destruction is where we will remain. I was caught up on the worldly things and split between God taking my pain away and me bearing my daughter's. I'm glad to say God came to my rescue and I've decided that He gets all the glory.

Isaiah 61:7 promises, "Instead of your shame

you will receive a double portion,
and instead of disgrace
you will rejoice in your inheritance.
And so you will inherit a double portion in your land,
and everlasting joy will be yours." (NIV)

Jeremiah 29:11, KJV translation states,
"For I know the thoughts that I think toward
you, saith the Lord, thoughts of peace, and
not of evil, to give you an expected end."

God gets All the Glory because He deserves it. Not to mention, it could've been worse.

WHILE IN THE VALLEY

As I was going through the dark times in my life, I was in the valley where I couldn't see. At times I could've ended my life over things of the world that I was going through.

While in the valley I begin to call on God who I thought had forgotten about me because of what I had done and had gone through in my past.

Psalm 23:4 Even though I walk through the valley of the shadow of death, I will fear no evil, for you are with me; your rod and your staff, they comfort me. (ESV)

While in the valley I battled with demons that I was fighting, and the fight wasn't for me it was the Lord the whole time. So when I got tired of losing the fight between myself and God I laid down in green pastures and let the Lord be my Shepard because I was his sheep and let the Lord wash me. He promised me if I let go and let him, he would watch over and protect me and help me get over trials and tribulation. At that time, God begin to restore my soul and lead me in the path of righteousness to get my mind, body, and soul right with the Holy Spirit.

While in the valley of darkness I found light and a man that gave me his unchanging hand I surrendered and reached my hands out to receive it to get everything the devil told me that I couldn't have.

God will always step in to make something out of nothing. He is our Alpha and Omega our beginning and the end I came out of darkness with my hands up and a praise and I am never going back to where I was. While in darkness God was able to shine his light upon me to bring me out of some things like hatred, bitterness, anger, rejection, abandonment, etc. All while I was in the valley.

WHEN YOU ARE SEEKING GOD FOR A CHANGE

Growing up as a child without a father was kind of hard for me. My sister and brothers' fathers were active in their lives, but not mine. My daddy wasn't worth two cents. He was in and out of jail. He was married to another woman, and my mom's choices didn't make it any easier. She had four different baby daddies, but my oldest brother's father was more active in his life and took good care of him. Every summer, my brother would go and stay with his father. I wanted that kind of relationship too. I can remember asking my mom why I couldn't go with my brother and his father, and it was the same with my other brother that was the knee baby's daddy.

My load was heavy, and I was so weighted down from all I endured living with my mom. That time of my life was so hard between wanting a father's love and attention and having a mother that was still upset with me because my baby sister's father was the one responsible for my molestation. It seemed like she was angry at me instead of him. So, she barely wanted me to stay there. She would always tell me I wasn't supposed to be here because my father raped her. In my mind, I was birthed out of violation because that is what she constantly told me. This negativity greatly affected me as a child.

When I grew up, I begin to search for love that wasn't and hadn't been given to me by my mother nor my father. I was forced to live where I could until God sent the first guy that I fell in love with. I remember being pregnant with my only child and thinking to myself, "This man here was different, not perfect but different." He provided me and my child with a home. He worked and sold drugs to see about us, but little did I know he had issues. His issues included cheating, telling lies, using drugs, being addicted to the streets, and his friends.

Now, I must be completely honest with you. My father would deal with me sometimes, but he really didn't know how because his drug addiction ran his life.

When I got with my husband, he was also a drug dealer. I used to hear so much about my father being a crackhead, and my cousin and siblings use to make fun of me about it, but I didn't know if it was true. Until one night, my father came home for a family member's funeral. He came to my home, acting like he was there to see me, but ended up outside with my husband and his friend. Boy, I was furious when I peeked out the window and saw my husband give my father some dope. Just to make sure I saw it correctly, I asked my husband, and Lord knows he didn't want to tell me the truth, but he did.

After that night, I didn't see my father anymore until one day he came by my home asking for a blood test. He was like I know you are mine, but this is to keep my license. If you are my child, then I owe back child support for twenty-seven thousand dollars, and I would have to give that to you. I was so confused. I told him that I didn't want his money and It didn't matter if he was my father or not. I went on to tell him that I didn't need a father; I had God.

See, I never wanted to feel how I felt about my dad, but I did and Although I decided to seek God for change, I had all this anger built up inside of me from both parents. As far as I was concerned, they both left me in darkness.

Well, my father passed away February 10, 2018, and It did something to me because a week before he passed away, I told him that if he died, I wouldn't shed a tear. At that time, I was walking with God, but I had not completely surrendered myself to him because I still had so much bitterness towards my dad. It was built up within me so much that it wouldn't let me be great. The night he passed; I was at a Church service. I began to shout and give God praise, and in that moment of praise, God told me my daddy said he loved me, and he was sorry for not being there. After service, my cousin called me from New York and informed me that my dad had passed. I threw up, cried, and threw up some more.

See, when moms bring us girls in the world, we do lean on having a father in our life. We need that, so I had to learn to lean on God to be a father and a mother to me.

While seeking God for change I learned to lean on God, and that is the best thing we can ever do. The damages in our lives that we go through are not because God has left us, but the enemy has tricked us into thinking that way. It is a trick of the enemy to think we are not worth being here.

So many times, I use to wish that I was dead because I didn't know how to live. I didn't know what it was like to be loved because I didn't love myself. My temple (body) was so unclean. I didn't have the mind of Christ. The enemy had me bound with the shackles were on my feet. While seeking God for change, I was broken gracefully, but I thought there wasn't any point of return.

"He restoreth my soul: he leadeth me in the paths of righteousness for his name's sake." "Yea, though I walk through the valley of the shadow of death, I will fear no evil: for thou art with me; thy rod and thy staff they comfort me." (Psalm 23:3-4, King James Version)

Psalm 23:3-4 reminded me of how God takes care of you when your light doesn't seem to shine. He is your light. Take the time to let these verses soak in. Memorize them if you must but keep them close.

Just imagine yourself, not even knowing how to pray. When you were growing up you was faithful in Church every Sunday. I remember being in the choir, being the Church secretary, and doing the welcome. I thought as long as I went to Church and still do wrong then God will forgive me because he knew my heart. Can somebody say, WRONG? A personal relationship with God is necessary. Yes, the Church is made up of people, but you must start with you because you are the Church. You got to learn how to pray for yourself. As long as you got other people praying for you it's not helping you to spiritually grow, yourself.

I knew God. I knew how to read the Bible and all, but I would get high. I would be at home reading John chapter fourteen and every time I would be praying that God didn't take me before I wake up. Honestly, I did this for years. I would beg God to take the taste out of my mouth. It seemed like the more I prayed this prayer the more drugs I did and alcohol I drank. If I had wings, I would've flown away from it all but in God's word Psalm 91:4-6 God reminded me to trust HIM with everything. So, I trusted Him with my reckless behavior and all my addictions.

Psalm 91:4-6 assures, "He shall cover thee with his feathers, and under his wings shalt thou trust: his truth shall be thy shield and buckler. 5Thou shalt not be afraid for the terror by night; nor for the arrow that flieth by day; 6Nor for the pestilence that walketh in darkness; nor for the destruction that wasteth at noonday." (King James Version)

Although I was seeking God for change, overcoming what I had going on in my life didn't happen overnight. I believe God sent me a Prophetess, my spiritual advisor to keep me grounded and rooted in God's word. There were many days and night of tears because I was so thirsty for God. I was tired of myself, while doing the same, and living the same.

See, I had voodoo put on me to kill me in my spirit. The lady that was responsible was intending on me losing my mind, but GOD turned it around and let me live spiritually for Him. If I hadn't surrendered to God, what the enemy had sent out for me to die would've worked. I thank God that He is a God of second chances.

I truly thank God for allowing me to marry my best friend on July 6, 2011. I'm so glad that when the enemy tried to destroy it, he failed because God ordained it to be. Mark 10:9 guarantees, "Therefore what God has joined together, let no one separate." (New International Version) Through our trials and tribulations, God did it. I stayed in my prayer closet and on my knees.

While seeking God for change, we will have to fast, pray, trust, believe, and obey. If God said it, you better believe it is already done. In spite of what I went through in this old life of mine, God continues to say to me, "You shall live and not die. You are a woman of God, you will speak in many tongues, you will lay hands only if I lead you to heal the sick and save souls."

At times, it gets worse before it gets better, but you must go through the fire and come out not smelling like smoke. Most Christians don't like to suffer while in the kingdom of God. Jesus suffered, so what makes us any better? It takes going through to get to your greater with the Holy Spirit as your guide.

In God's word, Jesus promises we will do greater works than him. John 14:12 confirms, "Verily, verily, I say unto you, He that believeth on me, the works that I do shall he do also; and greater works than these shall he do; because I go unto my Father." (King James Version)

Living our lives for Christ is not easy, but it is well worth it. I thank God that my mom didn't get rid of me. I wouldn't have had a chance in this life to get it right, to learn, be trained by God on how to walk like a servant, to think like the spirit, and to give love how God so loved the world that He gave His only begotten Son to save an unworthy woman like me. God made me worthy and no one can take that from me. Broken, but not damaged. I was healed. My issues were myself.

Are your issues, you? It was the root of me. Sometimes it takes you to be isolated to deal with what God is trying to do for you and in you. I thank God for my family, those that GOD removed and those that he allowed to stay.

While seeking God for change, I learned to keep him first in everything I do. I love God like no other. I pray that anyone that is going through anything reach out to God. Seek Him first and everything else will be added.

Don't give up on God. I know you want to throw in the towel but take that towel and use it to wipe yourself down. Wipe away all of the bitterness, pity, anger, jealousy, heartbreak, child molestation, and your wife/husband leaving you. Wipe it down, put it under your feet, stomp it out, and command it to be gone. Old things pass away, and God brings new things in a better day. The rain comes to wash away tracks of the past. The sun shines to dry you out and put light in the darkness of your life.

What happened had to happen. I believe God gives his toughest battles to his strongest soldiers. When you think you are weak, that is when you are at your strongest in God. God knows best. I am who I am today because God first loved me. If he did it for me, He will most definitely do it for you. Don't give out nor in, the enemy has no room. God is evicting him from your marriage, your finances, your children, your family, your friends, your mind, and your spirit.

This reminds me of the woman with the issue of blood. She suffered for twelve years, but when she learned to push her way through, she knew if she could stretch her hand far enough to touch the hem of his garment, she would be made whole. You need to hear me. Some of us need to push and press our way closer to God and be made whole again.

I leave this with you, seek God for change, take up your bed, and follow Jesus. He can make everything alright. No, it won't be sunshine every day, but if you start to thank God in it you will see brighter days.

Isaiah 60:19 encourages, "The sun will no more be your light by day, nor will the brightness of the moon shine on you, for the LORD will be your everlasting light, and your God will be your glory." (New International Version)

MY PAIN HAD PURPOSE

I remember not knowing what God had in store for me with things constantly going on in my life. It was a struggle to find a job, my marriage was on the rocks, and my family was falling apart. I lost two of the greatest friends I ever had. I experienced so much pain until I just wanted to give up on life. I wanted to throw in the towel and just walk away from it all. I gave my life to God, and I thought it was going to get easier, but it got worse.

One day, God spoke these words to me, "When you do my will, the greater level, the bigger the devil. You know that nothing comes easy, and you must go through the fire." I said to God, "Why me?" He replied, "Why not you, what makes you better than my Son, Jesus Christ?" On that day, I realized that my pain had a purpose.

I begin to read my word and seek God on the revelation of the Bible. I begin to listen to my spiritual advisor and sat with her daily as God spoke through her to me to give me scriptures that would help get me to where God was taking me. Along the way, I would lose some people not because I was better, but because where God was taking me, they weren't ready to go.

Gradually doors begin to open, and I started out as a housekeeper at Phoebe Putney and was suffering. I would get weary, but I continued to pray and listen to the Holy Spirit. I used to have to steal away from it all sometimes to cry. God would wipe my tears, and I would come out strong. This went on for two years and three months, and each day I would get stronger. I would walk around and push that cart, and what I could hear God say was you got to move. I was standing in the hallway of the hospital, and I told my brother in law, which was my supervisor that I was going back to school. I told him that I was going to get my certified nursing assistant certificate, and He looked at me and said, "You are not going to do nothing but go clean them rooms." I couldn't believe what he said to me, and I told him, "God said it, and I believed it."

I worked in housekeeping another week, and then God made a way. I was able to walk in there, turn in my uniforms and tell them I quit, while my other manager was trying to write me up. That was the funniest thing to me. I said to her again, "I QUIT, here is your badge, uniforms, and keys." Then, I walked out like Aibileen Clark on the Help, and I didn't look back. I stepped out on faith, not knowing what I was going to do because that was leaving my husband to foot all the bills by himself, but I knew I served a never failing God, and he made it feel so right.

In March of 2016, I started my C.N.A. class. I had a wonderful teacher that took time with her students to learn and pass. That May, I received my certification as a certified nursing assistant. See, I had been certified before while I was in school, but I had got into so much trouble that I lost my certification. I was so scared to try things because the enemy always used to say to me(self) you can't get a better job. You will never work in the nursing field. So, I remained tricked for almost 17 years.

During that time, I worked as a Patient Care Technician for Homehealth and had convinced myself that I was a C.N.A. for years. My husband would always tell me to go back to school, but I would always go against it. I would say I am not going to school, and I don't want to be like everyone else. I did that for years. My pain had a purpose. I became a full-time worker as a C.N.A. at a nursing home facility working double shifts and loving it. I went back to Phoebe Putney and got a job working on the floor as a C.N.A. so, I could watch the ones that said I wouldn't and encourage the girls that were still in housekeeping that they could do it too. Many of them left stepping out on faith and became a C.N.A. Some of them now are Registered Nurses because I unselfishly gave them the push & press God instilled in me. I poured out into others what God placed in me to pour for His glory.

Several years later, in April of 2019, I went back to school to become a Phlebotomist with the same teacher of New Beginnings and graduated obtaining my certification. I now work as a Phlebotomist. I minister to over 500 people that God has given to me. I put my marriage in God's hands, and nine years later, I'm still, He still, we still are THE Jay's Way.

See, we all experience pain in life. Whether it is emotional or physical pain, No pain is alike. We must all walk the journey and path that God has for our lives, yet God promises that there is a purpose in all pain. You can press on each day knowing that our God loves us unconditionally, and He wants to use the hurt and pain in this world that comes up against us to bring Him glory.

Jeremiah 29:11 states, "For I know the plans I have for you," declares the Lord, "plans to prosper you and not to harm you, plans to give you hope and a future." (NIV)

Psalm 147:3 assures us, "He heals the brokenhearted and binds up their wounds." (NIV)

Always remember God doesn't put you through suffering without a goal.

RECOVERY ROOM

Pain expands your endurance.

Pain matures you.

Pain teaches you what pleasure never could.

From all the scars, the beat downs, and the let downs, I can tell you about the pain. Pain is the price for a greater reward.

In the recovery room is where you feel better fast. It is where you gather all of what you just went through, but it wasn't unto the death of you.

As I was sitting with God one day, He began to minister to me about the recovery room, which is also called a post-anesthesia care unit (PACU). It is a space where a patient is taken after having surgery to safely regain consciousness from anesthesia and receive the appropriate post-operative care.

See, God told me, during my season of going through so much pain, suffering, and time, he placed me in the recovery room. See, through all our pain, scars, the scandalizing of our names, the suffering, tears, and more tears, we didn't know how we were coming out. So, while in the recovery room, you may experience a little nausea and some pain, but your medication is the word of God. There is no one welcome in there but you, the Father, the Son, and the Holy Spirit. During recovering from all of this, you may be a little disoriented when you do regain consciousness of what you have been through, but your wounds will be healed by God's stripes.

In the recovery room, you will be kept under strict supervision to make sure that you will walk out of the procedure better than you walked in, never to question again, "why you?" God said, "Why not you?" See, your healing process can't be rushed. You must have time to heal. Your process in the recovery room determines how you will come out. God is the doctor that has never lost a case. Stay in the recovery room with him. You must have time to heal. You can't heal others, if you don't heal, yourself.

MY PRAYER FOR FATHERLESS DAUGHTERS AND SONS

I pray that God gives you peace in your heart. Whether your natural father is deceased or if he is still on earth or whether he is in your home and you still didn't get the love that a father should have given you. I pray that you forgive them. I pray that you let God guide you to be better within yourself not what you went through but what God brought you out of; forgive them even if you were abused by someone you looked up to as a father, forgive them. It is not for them; it is for you. I pray that you let the Spirit fall on you and guide you to your greater because if you dream it, you can achieve it.

I pray that God dries your late-night tears and turn them into early morning joy. I pray that you know that even though you are fatherless that you know that you have a father that knows you, and that is our Father in Heaven. He will never leave you nor forsake you. I pray that each time you feel like you will never amount to anything that your mind be renewed and your vision be birthed to live, and you be connected to the right people through God that will receive your hope again.

Father God, in the name of Jesus, I pray this prayer reaches one and teaches one all over the world to know that if they woke up, they still have a chance to live and complete the tasks you have written and assigned to their lives. Father God, in the name of Jesus, touch their hearts with forgiveness towards their natural father. Fix how their mother made them feel about them. Father God, guide them, wrap your arms around the lost souls and bring them back to you because they are yours. Hallelujah. I pray. Amen

MY PRAYER FOR YOU

Father God, in the name of Jesus, I come to you as humble as I can be and give you all the glory for this amazing journey that you have me on. Some days are good. Some days are bad, but God, I thank you for my good always outweighs my bad. Father God, in the name of Jesus, I give you my yes to do your will and not my own. I pray that my story touches someone's life to let them know you did it for me, and you will do it for them.

Lord God, you say in your word, if we would stand on every word you say, you will begin to heal, and return everything back that the enemy stole. Lord God, as I come to an end, I know that it is only the beginning of this amazing life of mines that you have created just for me. I say thank you, Lord, for all you have done for me. When I wasn't worthy, God, you made me worthy and placed me up under you. Thank You, God, for loving me when I couldn't find a way to love myself. Thank you for always sitting high and looking low. I will never put any man above you.

I thank you, God, for my husband, my daughter, my mother, my sisters, and my brother. I thank you, God, for when they couldn't see what things you were doing in my life. I never hung my head low because I know every step that I made you were right there, moving every stumbling block out of my way. Hallelujah, in Jesus name, I pray Amen

ABOUT THE AUTHOR

Prophetess Shwana Jay is a devoted minister of the Lord. She is a devoted wife and the mother of one child.

Shwana gave her life to God at an early age and has struggled on this journey. She was in and out of the Church, until one day she decided to surrender it all to the Father.

She founded an organization called Sisters of Strength in 2013. This is an organization where she continues to reach out to young ladies to inspire, educate, and encourage them.

She received her certification as a C.N.A., and then later, Prophetess Jay acquired her certification as a Phlebotomist.

She was ordained as a Prophetess in 2017 to intercede and prophesy the word of God. Prophetess Shwana Jay is very ambitious and very determined. She is driving with a vision to always succeed with God guiding the way, and according to his will. Her degree in ministry is from the Lord to worship and warfare for people around the world.

Made in the USA
Columbia, SC
12 November 2023

25926622R00039